Will's Winning Ways

Story by Michael Pryor

Illustrations by Giuliano Aloisi

Will's Winning Ways

Text: Michael Wagner

Publishers: Tanya Fazeo and Eliza Webb
Series consultant: Amanda Sutera
  Hands on Heads Consulting
Editor: Beth Browne
Project editor: Annabel Smith
Designer: Jess Kelly
Project designer: Danielle Maccarone
Illustrations: Giuliano Aloisi
Production controller: Renee Tome

NovaStar

Text © 2024 Cengage Learning Australia Pty Limited
Illustrations © 2024 Cengage Learning Australia Pty Limited

ISBN 978 0 17 033413 6

Cengage Learning Australia
Level 5, 80 Dorcas Street
Southbank VIC 3006 Australia
Phone: 1300 790 853
Email: aust.nelsonprimary@cengage.com

For learning solutions, visit **cengage.com.au**

Printed in China by 1010 Printing International Ltd
1 2 3 4 5 6 7 28 27 26 25 24

*Nelson acknowledges the Traditional Owners and Custodians
of the lands of all First Nations Peoples. We pay respect
to Elders past and present, and extend that respect to
all First Nations Peoples today.*

Contents

Chapter 1

You Again, Will!

Towards the end of basketball training, Will liked to show everyone how good he was.

"Hey, watch this!" he called out to his teammates for about the hundredth time. He dribbled the ball from the centre circle, stopping briefly then jumping as he threw it towards the basket.

But instead of going in, the basketball hit the edge of the backboard and flew off at an angle.

With a crash, the ball landed on the bench where Ethan was lining up cups of drinks for Raj, Finn and the others. Sticky drink flew everywhere.

"Whoops," Will said.

But that wasn't all. The basketball bounced
into the storeroom with a bang. Basketballs
tumbled out of the storeroom, as the coach,
Ms Lee, came out of her office.

Ms Lee took one look at her dripping team.
"Don't tell me," she said. "It was you
again, Will!"

Will shrugged. "I was practising my power lay-up. Here, Coach, I'll try again."

Ethan and the others shook their heads. Ms Lee held up a hand. "I think we've had enough. Come with me, Will."

Chapter 2

A Serious Talk

Ms Lee took Will into her office. "Take a seat," she said. "It's time for a serious talk."

"It's okay, Coach," Will said. "I know you need me to show more classy moves to the team to inspire them and stuff like that."

Ms Lee shook her head. "Listen, Will. This season you've punctured three basketballs by trying to balance them on a fork. You broke the school speaker system with some wild karaoke nonsense. And you even ruined the team mascot costume."

Will snorted in disbelief. "How was I supposed to know that Tony Turtle's shell was so fragile? I thought I could slide across the court on it, no problem!"

"That's what I mean, Will," Ms Lee said. "You're always showing off, and you don't think of anyone else. That's why I'm going to suspend you from the team for the rest of the season."

"What?" Will jumped to his feet. "You can't do that! I'm the best player. The team will never win without me!"

"Maybe, maybe not," Ms Lee said, crossing her arms. "I'm sorry, Will, but that's my final decision."

Will stormed out of Ms Lee's office and nearly tripped over Ethan, who was mopping the court after everyone else had gone home. "I'm suspended from the team!" Will cried.

Ethan kept mopping. "Really?"

Will was angry. He complained as he followed Ethan around, while Ethan finished cleaning and packing up the equipment.

Finally, Will frowned. "I don't understand, Ethan. You're not always chosen for the team, so why are you doing all this stuff?"

Ethan wiped up the last of the sticky mess. "I might not always get a game, but I'm still part of the team." He shrugged. "So, I do what I can."

Will stared at him. "Even if you don't get a game?"

"Even if I don't get a game," Ethan agreed. "Teams are about more than just the game."

Chapter 3

Another Chance

Will still turned up to training, even though he was suspended. He loved basketball too much to stay away. But on the sidelines, he was bored. He started helping Ethan put out the drinks, mop the court, pack up the equipment and do all the other things a team needs that he'd never really thought about before.

The team started to win games, and it looked like they were going to reach the finals. Will felt grumpy. He wanted to be out on the court, showing what he could do. But Ethan encouraged him to keep pitching in. And the more Will did, the less grumpy he felt. He started to give tips to Finn on how to shoot a basket. He showed Raj how to fake a pass then throw it.

When Ethan started to get some time on the court, Will cheered louder than anyone. Even though he wasn't playing, Will felt like he was helping the team win. And when the team made the grand final, he was the first to high-five everyone.

At the training session the day before the grand final, Will was full of encouragement. "Slick lay-up, Raj!" he cried. "Cool passing, Finn! Nice dancing, Tony Turtle!"

Later, when Ethan sank his fifth long three-pointer in a row, Will whooped. "Go Ethan! You're the long-range goal-shooting master!"

Then Raj landed badly and rolled an ankle.
His face was twisted with pain.

"It's not good," Ms Lee said, after Raj's
parents took him to the hospital. "He
won't be able to play in the big game
tomorrow." She nodded at Will. "Come to
my office."

Ms Lee sighed. "I want you to take Raj's place on the team," she said to Will.

Will grinned. Even though he was sad for Raj, he was ready for this. "Because I'm the best player and I can win the game for you?" he asked.

"No," Ms Lee said, "because lately you've shown that you are part of the team, even though you haven't been playing."

Chapter 4

The Big Game

The stadium was packed for the grand final. Every seat was filled. Tony the Turtle danced and jumped around in his new costume.

The game started, and it was close from the first moments. The cheering after every goal was so loud, the whole stadium shook.

By the end of the first half, Will's team was doing well. But in the second half, the other team got in front.

Will was worried. The rest of his team were getting tired. Slowly, though, they started playing better and stopped the opposition scoring while making good baskets themselves.

In the last few seconds of the game, Will's team was one point behind, when Will grabbed the ball after an opposition player fumbled.

The crowd roared. Will was a long way from the basket, but he was feeling sure he could take the shot. It would be difficult, but if he was lucky, he could do it.
He could be the hero!

Then Will saw Ethan. He'd snuck past the opposition players, and he was closer to the basket than Will was. Ethan was still a long way out, but Will had seen him sink baskets from there.

Will whipped the ball to Ethan, and Ethan took it in both hands. For a second, he steadied. Then he took the shot. The ball went in, just before the buzzer sounded. The crowd went wild!

Will ran to Ethan. With the help of Finn, he chaired Ethan off the court while the stadium echoed with cheers and stomping.

Will was happy, even though he wasn't the one in the spotlight. He was back on the team – and the team had won!